FOUR STAGES OF SPIRITUAL GROWTH

From Infancy to Fathers

Maurice K. Wright

Rapier
PUBLISHING COMPANY

Unless otherwise indicated, all scriptures are from the King James Version

Scripture verses depicting KJV (King James Version), NASB (New American Standard Bible), Message Bible, Amplified Bible and the American Standard Versions Bible are taken from the Joyce Myers Ministries Bible Software: The Everyday Life Bible Study Library, WORDSearch, 2009. All rights reserved.

Four Stages of Spiritual Growth: From Infancy to Fathers

Copyright © 2014 by Maurice K. Wright (bishopmwright@bellsouth.net)

ISBN 978-0-9839483-3-9

Library of Congress Control Number 2014933719

Published by
Rapier Publishing Company
3417 Rainbow Parkway
Rainbow City, Alabama 35906
www.rapierpublishing.com

Printed in the United States of America

All rights reserved under the International Copyright Law. Contents and/or cover may not be reproduced in whole or in part in any form without the consent of the Publisher, or Author.

Book Cover Design: TimBen Graphics

Book Layout: Rapture Graphics

DEDICATION & ACKNOWLEDGEMENTS

I want to say first thanks to the Lord God Almighty who has inspired within me the desire to write. I have been moved by the Holy Spirit to write this discipleship-training book. Also, I want to thank my wife (Brenda) and my family for their love, patience and endurance throughout these years of ministry in the Lord. They have been my number one fans and support. I want to thank my spiritual father in the ministry, Apostle Halton (Pastor Alicia) Horton and the 7000 More Covenant Fellowship. You always encourage us to use our gifts, talents and abilities for the sake of the Kingdom. I want to thank Elders Bobby L. Garrett and Glenda Taylor for their thoughts, ideas and input as I shared my heart and vision with them. Last of all, I must say a very big thank you to the beloved United Christian Church Community of believers in Yeshua. You have believed in me and stuck by me through it all. Love and thanks to all!

FOREWORD

As Father of the 7000 More International Covenant Fellowship, it is with great pleasure to have a true son of God write such an inspiring and informative book that explains the word of God with such clarity. There are a few chosen men of God with the special gift of being able to teach the word of God which will impact and change your life, and it's found in Apostle Maurice K. Wright. Apostle Wright has written this book "The Four Stages of Spiritual Growth" from his heart, and he has lived and experienced each stage. As you read this book and assess your life from the infant stage to the mature stage as a father (neither male nor female in Christ Jesus) you will be able to learn from your oppositions and turn them into opportunities. Remember maturing in the Lord is a process of growth and development as you move toward the goal of more than enough. Congratulations to Apostle Wright for a well-thought-out book of life's true experiences.

Great Expectations,

Apostle Halton "Skip" Horton
The Day Star Tabernacle International
Douglasville, Georgia

AUTHOR's COMMENTS

To illustrate to you the process of progression in maturity, let us use the baseball field diagram depicted below. It has four basses: first base, second base, third base and home plate

The object of the game is to score runs. In order to score a run the game has rules that each player must adhere to. The rules of the game state that you must go through all the bases in order, from first to third base, and then to home plate. You cannot score without going to each base.

The object is not just to get on base, but it is to progress from base to base until you reach home plate, and this has to be done in order. You cannot go from first base across the field to third, because this goes against the rules, second base cannot be overlooked.

It is the same in the spirit realm for the children of God. Yes, you do want to get on base (first). You cannot score a run unless you get on base. But we cannot become content or totally satisfied with just being on base. You should want to score. In the diagram, below we have provided for you what each base represents in the spiritual growth game: First base (infancy), second base (childhood), third base (young man) and home plate (adult, fathers).

God is pleased when we get on base through salvation. However, He desires to see those who get on base come to maturity in fatherhood in the Lord.

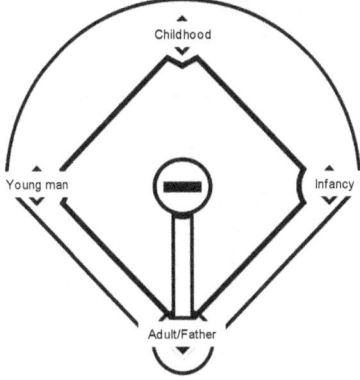

Now that you are on base! SCORE!

TABLE OF CONTENTS

Preface..11

Objective..15

Introduction: The Four Stages of Spiritual Growth....................19

Stages Overview...23

Spiritual Growth Stages Traits..27

Stage One: Infant Stage (Provision Stage).............................31

Stage Two: Childhood Stage (Identity Stage).........................37

Stage Three: Young Men Stage (Awareness Stage)................43

Stage Four: Father/Adult Stage (Trusting Stage)....................49

Conclusion..53

Notes..55

References..58

PREFACE

As I prepare this teaching to assist the body of Christ, the Church, in their personal spiritual growth and path to spiritual maturity, I am reminded of the words of Yeshua [Jesus] to the Pharisees. He said, "Woe to you, scribes and Pharisees, hypocrites! For you tithe ... and have neglected the weightier provisions of the law: justice and mercy and faithfulness; but these are the things you should have done without neglecting the others" (Matthew 23:23, NASB).

Here, Jesus reprimanded these religious leaders for majoring in the lesser things or responsibilities of the Kingdom of God, which as believers, saints, disciples, and citizens of the Community of believers in Christ Jesus should be our focus, or priority. "They were remarkably scrupulous in the performance of all the rites and ceremonies of religion, but totally neglected the spirit, soul, and practice of godliness."[1]

Jesus said, "These ought ye to have done." "Our Lord did not object to their paying tithe even of common pot-herbs—this did not affect the spirit of religion; but while they did this and such like, to the utter neglect of justice, mercy, and faith, they showed that they had no religion, and knew nothing of its nature."[2]

The main point in this passage is that one should properly order one's priorities- to put first things first (without totally neglecting the other required things of lesser importance), and live a life pleasing to God.

Too many believers in Christ Jesus have failed to take personal responsibility for their own spiritual growth and maturity. They begin with great excitement and joy about being saved, but lack the

---

1 Matthew 23:23, Adam Clark Commentary.
2 Ibid.

discipline, devotion and determination needed to reach the level of maturity that God, the Father desires and will for every child of His to attain. As a result, the Church has been hindered, and not as effective or mobile as she should because of the immaturity and carnality that make up a great percentage of the Church. Hence, it is not a question of our salvation, but a question of our maturity.

This immaturity is a part of the curse of "having no fathers" (Malachi 4:5-6). The Church is in great need of true spiritual fathers to teach, train, mentor, and prepare the next generation and sons of God for greater work and more effective service in the Lord. *See – II Timothy 2:1-2.* We still need fathers in the Lord, who have been called, chosen and anointed by the LORD. Fathers who God can and will use "to turn" many men hearts to their God and Savior. Fathers who will go forth in the spirit and power of Elijah as servants and witnesses for Christ, turning the hearts of the fathers back to the children, and the disobedient to the attitude of the righteous; so as to make ready a people prepared for the Lord" (Luke 1:15-17 Amplified Bible).

It is the will of God the Father in heaven that once a sinner comes to Christ, confesses Jesus Christ as Lord, receives the gift of salvation and the indwelling of the Holy Spirit through faith by grace, and really taste of the goodness and kindness of the Lord, he or she grows up in his or her salvation and comes to full maturity and complete knowledge of God.

Therefore, let us eliminate any and every excuse we have or have used for our lack of spiritual growth and immaturity as the "children" and "sons" of God. Please, no more excuses or procrastination! Let's go, grow, and glow with the glory of God, reflecting the very nature, character and essence of our God to the world. We have been commanded to *"Let our light so shine so that men can see our good works and glorify our Father in heaven"* (Matthew 5:16). In other words, men should visibly see the work God is doing in the life of the believer/disciple, as he or she becomes a reflection of Him, because of the manifestation of Christ's life working daily in and through his or her life – to the glory of the Father.

Know that you and I are the only hope for the Church and our Community of believers in Jesus Christ being spiritual, mature, and effectively doing the greater works Jesus said His followers should do. The Church and your local congregation will only be as spiritual, mature, and effective as the people who make it up. Both God and the Church need every believer in Christ Jesus to grow spiritually and come to the full maturity in Christ.

IT IS HIS WILL...

OBJECTIVE

This particular teaching has a specific objective that we desire to accomplish in the end. Like Father God, we want to establish the end from the beginning, and end up where we desire to end up on purpose. We will not be surprised when we get there. It will be our intended end.

Here is our objective.

"To set in place an effective and established course of action that will assist every true believer and genuine disciple of Christ that will allow them to enter into the process of discipleship and spiritual growth that leads to maturity and a perfect (complete) man. This course of action will include a systematic planned curriculum that will teach each participant the four stages or levels of spiritual growth, as well as the need and importance of growth that leads to maturity. Our desire is to teach the truth with simplicity, clarity, and understanding."

Our goal is to instruct the saints of God in a more perfect way, and to help each one progress in the process with each new level they attain **UNTIL** the desired end is reached. What is the desired end? **MATURITY!**

We also desire to teach and train men and women who will know how to disciple and teach other potential disciples the stages and levels of growth. It is about duplication, reproduction, and mentoring.

"SO YOU, my son, be strong (strengthened inwardly) in the grace (spiritual blessing) that is [to be found only] in Christ Jesus.² And the [instructions] which you have heard from me along with many witnesses, transmit and entrust [as a deposit] to reliable and faithful men who will be competent and qualified to teach others also" (II Timothy 2:1-2, Amplified Bible).

It is our heart's desire and goal to effectively and efficiently help assist and guide every newborn babe in Christ, every under-developed and immature believer in the household and body of Christ, and every new member the Lord adds to the family and our Community of believers in Yeshua [Jesus] to grow or grow up in their salvation and walk with God.

Our goal is to see all the members of our household come to full maturity, and learn how to walk in the way of righteousness, to walk worthy of our vocation, and in all of the commandments of God. As each person remains and perseveres in the process toward the goal, we will seek to take them from _dependency_ to _independence_ to _interdependence_. **We desire to see every son of God and child in the household become a "self-feeder." That is, they become a genuine disciple of Christ, who is a student of Word; one who studies to show themselves approved as an unashamed workman unto God who knows how to spiritually discern all things and to rightly divide the Word of Truth. THEY WILL BE A WORSHIPER OF GOD, AND HAVE THEIR OWN PERSONAL INTIMATE RELATIONSHIP WITH GOD THE FATHER THROUGH JESUS CHRIST HIS SON, AND ENJOY DAILY SWEET COMMUNION AND FELLOWSHIP WITH THE HOLY SPIRIT OF GOD.** (II Corinthians 13:14)

Here are some things that I believe are the keys to spiritual growth and maturity in Christ:

1. Desire	1. Passion	1. Availability	1. Hunger
2. Discipline	2. Pursuit	2. Appetite	2. Humility
3. Devotion	3. Pain	3. Absolute (Resolve)	3. Hopeful

Remember, it is a **process** of **progression** that leads to **growth** and **maturity**.

PROCESS = means a systematic series of actions directed to some end; a continuous action or operation of changes taking place in a definite manner or order; the action of going forward or on.

PROGRESSION = means the act or state of forward or onward movement; a passing successively from one member of a series to the next; succession; sequence.

GROWTH = means the act or process, or manner of increasing gradually in size, statue, quality, amount, etc.; development; gradual increase; something that has grown or developed by a natural or spiritual process.

MATURITY = means the state of being mature or complete in natural or spiritual growth or development; ripeness; full development; possessing the characteristic of full development.

(*See Reference page on underlined words.)

INTRODUCTION

THE FOUR STAGES OF SPIRITUAL GROWTH

"I write unto you, little children . . ."

"I write unto you, fathers . . ."

"I write unto you, young men . . ."
(I John 2:12-14)

"And I, brethren, could not speak unto you as unto spiritual, but as unto carnal, even as unto babes in Christ."
(I Corinthians 3:1)

In I Corinthians chapter 15, verses 46 thru 49, the apostle Paul talks about both the natural and spiritual order of things. He said, "The natural was first, then that which is spiritual." That which is of the natural and is temporal belongs to the earth; and that which is spiritual and is eternal belongs to the heavenly.

There is a specific process of growth and development that a newborn baby has to go through in order to become a mature responsible adult in the natural. The process is the same for the (new) born-again infant child of God. It is just a spiritual process that produces spiritual growth and things. Remember, there are a natural order and realm, as well as a spiritual order and realm. The flesh produces fleshly results; whereas, the spirit produces spiritual results. See – <u>John 3:6; Galatians 6:8.</u> The newly born-again believer in Jesus Christ is a babe, an infant child, who has to go through the spiritual process or order to become a mature responsible adult or father in the Lord. **IT IS A PROCESS: A PROCESS OF GROWTH AND DEVELOPMENT AS ONE MOVE TOWARD THE GOAL -- <u>MATURITY</u>.**

The apostle Peter said, *"As newborn babies, long for the spiritual milk which is without guile, that ye may grow thereby unto salvation; if ye have tasted that the Lord is gracious"* (I Peter 2:2-3, ASV). In the natural, newborn babies come here with a natural desire or longing for milk! No parents have to teach their newborn baby how to crave milk or suck the breast. They are born with it. It should be and is the same way in the spiritual. Newborn babies in Christ, who have been born from above (John 3:1-5), should crave and long for the sincere pure milk of the Word of God, and long to taste more of the goodness and grace of the Lord Jesus Christ, their Savior and Lord.

Peter makes it perfectly clear that this is the beginning toward an end, as the believer who long for and drink the milk of the Word begins to grow up in their salvation and come to maturity in Christ. There should not be any prolonged infancy in the natural or spiritual. To grow is normal. To not grow is abnormal. There are two reasons why Christian fell to grow: (1) they don't want to grow; or, (2) they don't know how to grow. It is the will of the Father that every born-again child of His grows or grows up in his salvation and come to full maturity or perfection in Christ. See – <u>Hebrews 5:11-6:3; II Peter 3:18; Ephesians 4:11-16.</u>

Know that there will not be any spiritual growth without the Word of God. In every stage of the process to maturity, the Word of God must be a priority. It must continue to be read, heard, studied, memorized, cherished and applied. Man can only live by the words that have proceeded out of the mouth of God (Matthew 4:4). You have to commit to becoming a disciple and to have the discipline to read, hear, and study the Word of God.

Know also that it will not happen without the true believer and disciple of Jesus Christ having someone to teach and to instruct you in a more perfect way in the Lord. God has given us fathers and teachers, the ascension gifts of Christ, to teach us and help us come to full maturity (Ephesians 4:11-16; Acts 11:19-26; 14:21-23; 18:24-28).

However, know that it will not happen without being planted in and connected to a local fellowship, community or congregation of the Lord. You must assemble yourself in an assembly where the saints of God assemble for worship, praise, growth, service, hearing God's Word, receiving His instructions, receiving His blessings, making your contribution, and so on (Hebrews 10:24-25; Acts 2:38-48; Psalm 92:12-15). It requires both personal growth, study and development, as well as corporate growth, discipleship, and instructions.

No man is an island!

Iron sharpens iron! (Proverbs 27:17)

I am my brother's keeper! (Genesis 4:9)

STAGES OVERVIEW

Here are the four stages or levels of growth that every newborn babe, both naturally and spiritually, must go through:

1. *Infant Stage:* "Provision Stage" – You supply!
   INNOCENCE!

2. *Childhood Stage:* "Identity Stage" – You affirm!
   IMPRESSIONABLE/ INATTENTIVE!

3. *Young Man Stage:* "Awareness Stage" – They prove themselves (responsible & accountable)!
   INDEPENDENT!

4. *Father Stage:* "Trusting Stage" – Total confidence in God!
   INFLUENTIAL!

A. Infant Stage:

   1. Provide care & nurturing.

   2. Provide hands-on ministry.

   3. Provide a loving relationship that will foster healthy development & growth.

   4. Provide an atmosphere or environment conducive for the baby's well-being.

   5. Provide a lot of love & patience (here you will be required to give a whole lot of yourself lovingly, freely & willingly).

B. Childhood Stage:

   1. Identify: knowing & finding your identity in Christ; who you really are.

   2. Identify character flaws (that will hinder) your

development & growth.

3. Identify areas that need loving discipline & correction.
4. Identify the path their heart & life may be bent toward.
5. Identify their need for guidance because of their immaturity.

C. <u>Young Man Stage:</u>
1. Awareness (Simple/Natural).
2. Awareness of strength and weaknesses; harness flesh while dealing with & confronting weaknesses honestly & with total dependence upon God.
3. Awareness of character: modeling a godly character & being an example.
4. Awareness of acceptance [in Christ] and avoidance [of evil].
5. Awareness of adversary: identifying, recognizing, & overcoming the adversary.

D. <u>Father Stage:</u>
1. Relationships (Right).
2. Responsible (Accountability).
3. Restful Resolve.
4. Restorer/Repairer.
5. Rejoicing & Reward (a place of).

We will discuss each stage and what things and characteristics should be seen at each level and with each one. Each stage or level is necessary and cannot be skipped or neglected. There is something significant to be learned at every stage that will help prepare you for the next stage. In essence, you and I must take full advantage of each stage and what it brings and provides for us in the growth process.

Let us take a moment to define some key words or terms we will be using in the teaching manual.

<u>STAGE</u> = means a single step or degree in a process; a particular phase, period, position in a process; development or series.

1.) Notice that it is a single step and not many steps at one time.

2.) It is a specific position in the development or growth process.

3.) It is one step, one position, one phase at a time. Therefore, be patient, persistent, and purposeful in the development process to maturity.

<u>LEVEL</u> = means a position with respect to a given or specified height, status, or rank.

Whatever you do, don't rush the process but stay in the process! You will never reach or attain the goal if you do not stay in the process. Know where you are in the process and be true to yourself. Know where you want to go, but be honest about where you really are.

> "Learn how to enjoy where you are while you are on your way to where you are going."
>
> _____**Joyce Meyers**

*"And He was saying, 'The Kingdom of God is like a man who cast seed upon the soil; and goes to bed at night and gets up by day, and the seed sprouts up and grows – how, he himself does not know. The soil produces crops by itself; **first** the blade, **then** the head, **then** the mature grain in the head"*(Mark 4:26-28, NASB).

The Greek meaning of the word "mature"[3] here means "replete or covered over; (by analogy) complete: -- full." Figuratively speaking it means "full in the sense of being complete." "Spiritual growth is something that happens without visible cause. The parable in Mark here describes the divine-human act of believing and growing in grace. Just as the mystery of life (whether plant or animal) is unexplainable by man, so also the mystery of spiritual growth is ultimately unexplainable by man. It is the work of God's grace and the Holy Spirit through Christ."[4]

*"And when you enter the land and plant all kinds of trees for food, **then** you shall count their fruit as forbidden. **Three** years it shall be forbidden to you; it shall not be eaten. But in the **fourth** year all its fruit shall be holy, an offering of praise to the LORD. And in the **fifth** year you are to eat of its fruit, that its yield may increase for you; I am the LORD your God"* (Leviticus 19:23-25, NASB).

"Here the Israelites were not to pick the fruit from the trees planted in the Promised Land for three years. They were instructed not to eat the fruit from the trees too quickly. The fruit of the fourth year was to be offered and dedicated to the LORD, and in the fifth year the fruit could be eaten."[5]

This was the natural order given by the LORD for the eating of the fruit from the trees planted in the Promised Land. I believe we should approach the spiritual order the same way. We should not expect too much too soon from the newborn again babe in Christ. We do want to see them grow and become productive bearing much fruit to the glory of God (John 15:8). But we must not push or force them into ministry too soon, especially when they are immature and have not spiritually developed to be effective in ministry.

---

3 Strong Hebrew Greek

4 Mark 4:26-28, Adam Clark Commentary

5 MacDonald, p.157

SPIRITUAL GROWTH STAGES TRAITS

The following are distinguishing qualities, peculiarities, or inherited characteristics of each stage or level of growth and development on the way to the goal [MATURITY] as one move through the process. You will experience certain traits on the specific stage or level you find yourself in the process of progression.

INNOCENCE – THE BABY STAGE:

"Innocence" means "free from guilt, sin, reproach, or blame; it is one that is faultless and without condemnation; simplicity; one usually with innocent actions or qualities."

1.) Infants are in a state and stage of innocence.

2.) Infants are never condemned or judged.

3.) Infants are not aware of who they are yet, nor are they aware of their surroundings.

4.) Infants are free in a sense and possess freedom from cares and worry.

5.) Infants are usually free from guile and cunning.

> "A baby can't talk at all. When they try to communicate, it usually doesn't make sense."

IMPRESSIONABLE/INATTENTIVE–THE CHILDHOOD STAGE:

"Impressionable" means "capable of being transmitted to another or producing a vivid impression upon; a mark, action, act, image, etc. made or caused by an effect resulting from influence; an effect of alteration or improvement upon one by another."

"Inattentive" means "not attentive; failure to pay attention; unable to look after or give heed to; unable to apply the mind to an object of sense or thought; unable to apply the mind or pay attention: NOT ABLE TO HEED."

1.) Children do not have long attention spans.

2.) Children are not yet fully developed in mind and thought.

3.) Children have narrow focus of consciousness and receptivity.

4.) Children are an easy prey for deception because they are so easy to impress with candy, gimmicks, and games.

5.) Children can so easily develop and possess characteristics or traits from some influence, whether negative or positive.

"A Child talks like a Child."

INDEPENDENT – THE YOUNG MAN STAGE:

"Independent" means "not dependent; not subject to the control of others: SELF-GOVERING; not relying on or requiring something else; not looking to others for one's opinions or for guidance in conduct; showing a desire for freedom."

1.) A young man knows his or her identity and how they are capable of governing himself or herself without supervision.

2.) A young man knows that his or her path is directed by the LORD as he or she acknowledges Him in all of their ways and all of their days. They act on God's knowledge.

3.) A young man knows that he or she can move and flow with God and His will without always needing the opinions of others.

4.) A young man has the conduct and lifestyle of one who has been freed indeed by Christ, the Son of God.

5.) A young man knows his or her independence, but he or she also knows that they are a part of a body and community. Therefore, he or she knows that they are interdependent as well. They are related and connected to others.

"A Young Man (spiritually speaking) has put away childish things. He no longer speaks, thinks, or has the understanding of a child."

INFLUENTIAL – THE FATHER STAGE:

"Influential" means "exerting or possessing the act or power of producing an effect upon others without apparent exertion of force or direct exercise of command; the power or capacity of causing an effect, whether negative or positive, in indirect or intangible ways; the ability to sway or persuade others."

1.) Fathers are leaders who possess the ability and power to persuade others for good.

2.) Fathers are those who possess the power to produce results with grace.

3.) Fathers are nurturers who know how to raise their children in the admonition of the LORD without being forceful or pushy.

4.) Fathers are those who possess the peace of God and are unmoved and undisturbed by the situations and circumstances of life.

5.) Fathers are those who lead by example and who can have a positive effect upon people in indirect or intangible ways. They don't have to say anything or speak any words at certain times. They model righteousness and right action with their deeds, conduct, attitude, and lifestyle.

Fathers are those who are mature. They know how to be like a child when it comes to malice, but be a (mature) man when it comes TO UNDERSTANDING!

STAGE ONE:

INFANT STAGE (Provision Stage)

The *"infant stage"* is the first stage or step toward "maturity" or "fatherhood." One must walk out, cultivate and develop all the necessary qualities and characteristics of the present stage before he can move and go to the next stage in the process toward maturity. When one is born again, he is a "babe in Christ." Spiritually, he is an infant.

An *"infant"* is "a child during the earlier periods of his life, especially before he or she can feed himself or herself, walk, talk, etc.; anything in the first stage of existence or progress; being in infancy."

This is the stage where the parents, guardians or caretakers will have to do all the work and provide for the baby or infant needs. You will always be giving here. In a sense, the parent, caretaker, or guardian is the provider who is responsible for making provision for the infant or babe. "Provision" means "the supplying of something, especially of food or necessities; to make available or furnish the necessities; to prepare beforehand what is needed."

This babe or infant is the receiver. *"Receive"* means "to have (something) bestowed, delivered, or brought to one; to take into one's possession; to be burdened with; sustain." Many newborn babes in Christ have fallen through the cracks in our method or way of doing church; as a result, they fail to become disciples. Too often we have left these newborn again babes to provide and care for themselves. They need to be fed the milk of the Word by the spiritual overseers, who are responsible for the oversight of the household and the feeding of the sheep. To help them with this responsibility, they need those who are spiritually matured in the house to assist in the teaching and disciplining of others.

Here are five responsibilities or duties of the parental parents (eldership) and other qualified and trained disciples or spiritual saints in the house:

1. Provide care and nurturing.

    (a.) The babe in Christ will need to be supplied with the basic necessities for spiritual growth: <u>milk</u> and <u>love</u>. I Peter 2:2 says, *"Like newborn babies you should crave (thirst for, earnestly desire) the pure (unadulterated) spiritual milk, that by it you may be nurtured and grow unto [completed] salvation"* (Amplified Bible). Babies should never be left alone. They cannot feed or care for themselves. They must be loved first in order to return the love they receive. ***See – 1 John 4:19; <u>Ezekiel 16:1-19.</u>***

    (b.) In the infant stage, the baby will not have much to give the parents or caretakers; he or she only receives. The parents or caretakers must give and furnish the babe all that he or she needs at this stage.

    (c.) Nurturing involves more than just feeding. It includes "loving, protecting, rearing, supporting, upbringing, developing, educating, and encouraging; as during the period of training or development." Caring means "to give serious attention to; to be concern or have thought or regard for; to have an inclination or affection for."

2. Provide hands-on ministry!

    (a.) Babies have to be loved, fed, held, pampered, watched, cared for, etc.

    (b.) Babies have to be cleaned and washed up after they have made a mess on themselves. In this stage, we can expect babies to make a mess sometimes.

3. Provide a loving relationship that will foster healthy development and growth.

   (a.) Why do we love God? Because He first loved us (I John 4:19). Babies cannot love. They are the recipients or receivers of the love given and shown to them. As the babe grows in the natural and the spiritual and progress forward to the next stage of growth, they usually respond back in love to the love shown them.

   (b.) The parents or caretakers should never do anything that is unhealthy or ungodly that will impact and influence the baby in a negative way.

4. Provide an atmosphere or environment conducive for the baby well-being.

   (a.) It is the responsibility of the parents or caretakers to create and maintain the right kind of environment or atmosphere that will foster healthy spiritual and social growth; and that will guide the child in the way of righteousness. See – **_Genesis 18:19; Joshua 24:14-15; Luke 2:51-52._**

   (b.) It needs to be an atmosphere or environment of trust, love, patience, hope, worship, prayer, honesty, integrity, the fear of the Lord, etc.

   (c.) It must be a surrounding or pervading mood that is conducive for positive influence and godly living.

5. Provide a lot of love & patience (you will be required to give a lot here).

   (a.) The love given and shown to the child or children by the parents or caretakers should be unconditional, and without a sense of a burden. It should be a delight to care for your baby, God's baby. **_Children are the heritage of the LORD… and arrows in your hand (Psalm 127:3-4)._**

(b.) Parenting and caretaking require a whole lot of patience. You must never forget who you are nurturing, protecting, and caring for – A BABY. *They can't give much, but they need to receive a lot!*

> *Know that babies and children have to be* **weaned** *(Genesis 21:8; 1 Samuel 1:22-24; Psalm 131:2; Isaiah. 28:9).*
>
> **"No prolonged infancies among us, please. We'll not tolerate babies in the woods, small children who are an easy mark for impostors. God wants us to grow up, to know the whole truth and tell it in love – like Christ in everything"** **(Ephesians 4:14-15, Message Bible).**

The Jewish Boy Process to Pursuing a Calling:

The following is the process every Jewish parent followed in preparing their boy for answering the call of God. They were committed to keeping and obeying this pattern. (From the book: "Sitting at the Feet of Rabbi Jesus.")[6]

1. In his earlier years at home (infant to 4 years), he learns to recite the Shema found in Deuteronomy 6:4-9.

2. From the age of 5, he would have begun memorizing at least parts of the Hallel in Psalms 113-118.

3. When he is about 6, he would have been sent to the synagogue to learn reading and writing. The only textbook in an orthodox synagogue school was the Scriptures, which the Jews believed contained everything one needed to know about the world, whether in the realm of science, art, religion, or law.

4. At the age of 10, he would have begun memorizing large portions of the "traditions of the elders," orally transmitted teachings that would not be codified until A.D. 200 by

---

6 Spangler and Tverberg, p. 24-25

Judah ha-Nasi in Sepphan's, Galilee.

5. At the age of 12 or 13, he would have been given the rite of bar mitzvah (son of the commandment) or its ancient counterpart by the elders of the synagogue. You are declared an adult with this rite of passage.

> *The Jewish male begins to wear "tefillin" (Heb., prayer) at this point, or phylacteries. He may also wear the "tallit," or prayer shawl (Num. 15:37–41).*

6. At age 15, he would have begun in earnest to study the oral traditions that were later codified in the Talmud, which contained the Gemara in addition to the Mishnah.

7. At about the age of 18, a Jewish man was expected to marry, especially one who was training to be a rabbi.

8. At the age of 20, he would begin to pursue a calling.

9. Age 30 was considered to be the age of maturity when a man began his ministry. Both John the Baptist and Jesus was 30 when they began their ministries.

STAGE TWO:

CHILDHOOD STAGE (Identity Stage)

This is the stage where the child begins to look and desire his or her identity. It is at this stage that parents or caretakers begin to bend their child toward his or her identity: the way that they should go, and the behavior they should display when they become adults. A lot of time is spent here preparing them for life later as an adult and when they are walking and living independently apart from the parents or caretakers. Childhood stage is the development and training stage or level.

<u>Childhood</u> = the state of being childish or the period between infancy and youth; having the characteristics of a child.

<u>Development</u> = the act or process of bringing into being or evolving; bringing out the possibilities or capabilities; the act or process of causing something or someone to go through the process of natural or spiritual evolution from a previous and lower stage; the process of developing growth, progress; a developed state or form.

<u>Training</u> = the education, instruction, or discipline of a person or thing that is being strengthened or guided in the right direction.

<u>Identify</u> = to recognize or establish as being a particular person or thing; verify the identity of; to serve as a means of identification for.

1. Identity: know who you really are & your identity in Christ.

    (a.) Believers are now "the sons or children of God."

    (b.) Your identity is found in Christ and in the Word of God. It is only when you come to know who Christ is that you find your true identity in Him. You are who the Word says you are – not men. *(<u>John 1:12; Romans 8:29; Galatians 3:26-29; 4:1-7; 1 John 3:1-3.</u>)*

(c.) It is in Christ that we do three things according to Acts 17:28. In Christ Jesus we:

_____ = are alive, living, and have life in our lifetime;

_____ = go; stir around; go or walk in the way of life or the path of His choosing and predetermined purpose;

_____ = are, be, or exist for His purpose and glory; have hope. THE TRUTH OF THE MATTER IS THAT WE ONLY EXIST BECAUSE OF HIM AND HIS PURPOSE.[7]

2. Identify character flaws for development.

   (a.) It is the responsibility of the parents or caretakers to identify the features or defects that mar the perfection of the manifestation of the character and nature of Christ in and through our lives; a defect impairing the vision of the life of Christ within the believer. *(1 Thessalonians 2:1-12; Ephesians 6:1-4; 1 Corinthians 4:14-21; 2 Timothy 1:6-7; Proverbs 31:1-9.) We must also commend them on the good qualities we see too.*

   (b.) The sooner we can recognize these flaws and deal with them, the better it will be. We must not overlook and ignore character flaws and human weaknesses. They must be confronted and dealt with lovingly, with compassion and much patience; but we must also speak and make known the truth in love. *Proverbs 22:15 says, "Foolishness is bound up in the heart of a child; the rod of correction [discipline] will remove it*

---

[7] Gilbrant and Lint, p. 425

far from him" (NASB). The Word of God is a rod that can bring correction and change (2 Timothy 3:15-17). Young and old men or older believers are taught to flee youthful/childhood lusts (2 Timothy 2:22). They are called "childhood lusts" and are associated with that level. The remedy to lust is to flee: RUN.

3. Identify areas needing loving discipline & correction.

   (a.) Discipline is a manifestation of one's love for their child or children. However, discipline without relationship equals rebellion. It is almost impossible to discipline a child whom you do not have a relationship with.

   (b.) Discipline has great benefits and rewards. *Read – Hebrews 12:5-11.*

4. Identify the path their heart & life may be bent toward.

   (a.) Gifting, talent, abilities, calling, etc.: "Train up a child in the way he should go, even when he is old he will not depart from it" (Proverbs 22:6, NASB). Every child heart is not bent in the same way or path; they do not possess the same calling, gifts, talents, ability, skill, etc. *(Romans 12:3-6; Ephesians 4:7.)*

   (b.) Speech and vocabulary development *(1 Corinthians 13:11; Ephesians 4:29; Colossians 4:6):* Your word is your bond, and your speech says a lot about your character.

   - The creative power of your words; your confession of faith! *(Hebrews 11:3; 3:1; Mark 11:23)* The child hasn't yet learned that his or her words have creative power and ability. Words are powerful and creative too. You can be trapped by your own words (Proverbs 6:2).

   - Avoiding idle words! *(Matthew 12:33-37; Jeremiah 1:12)* Words reveal character! "Idle in the Greek means "inactive, i.e. unemployed; (by implication) lazy, useless: - barren, unfruitful, unproductive, slow, or words spoken with no purpose, aim, or intention."[8] Employ words and make them accomplish what you purposefully send them to do.

- Learning to say what you mean and mean what you say!

(c.) Choices and consequences:

- Making right choices: life is choice driven. *(1 Peter 3:8-13; 1 Chronicles 28:5-10.)* Only you are responsible for the words you speak. Watch your words or what you say, especially if they do not agree with the Word of God. Sometimes silence is golden, and a few words are grand.

- Know what you want to reap before you make any decision. *(Galatians 6:7-8.)* My spiritual father Apostle Halton "Skip" Horton often says, "You look like your decision."

(d.) Path of evil they may be easily tempted to follow and fall:

- There is a need to know one's weakness or dark side.

- Admit and acknowledge the obvious area(s) of vulnerability and weakness the person may be easily tempted to yield!

5. Identify their need for guidance because of their immaturity. *(Hebrews 5:11-6:3)*

---

8 Strong's Hebrew Greek Concordance

(a.) Children have foolishness in their hearts. They are immature. They possess some *"youthful lusts"* that come with just being a child.

(b.) Children do not know the way to take or the path to travel most of the time. You cannot leave some decisions to children. Spiritual children of the Lord sometimes do not always know the path to travel or the decision to make based upon the Word of God. They are usually inexperience in the Word of God at this stage and have a carnal mind.

(c.) Children are very impressionable, gullible, easily mislead, tossed too much by deceptive doctrines, and lack knowledge of their own value and the value of spiritual things.

STAGE THREE

YOUNG MEN STAGE (Awareness Stage)

This is the stage or level of *"awareness."* The older people had a saying when a young man or woman was beginning to be aware of their masculinity and femininity, especially when they begin to be really attractive to the opposite sex. They said, "He or she is beginning to smell himself or herself." In other words, he is becoming aware of his masculinity as a man, and of the things men desire to do, and she is becoming aware of her femininity, and of the things women desire to do.

As he or she becomes older and progresses closer to the fatherhood stage, the parents or caretakers will have to release their child to make certain decisions on their own, and to learn how to take responsibility for their choices and actions. They are no longer a child. Therefore, we must not treat them as a child and confined them with certain childhood restrictions. Of course, you do have to consider each child's ability to make certain decisions and to handle certain responsibilities, and how much they have developed thus far.

Let us look at these definitions as they pertain to this stage:

<u>Release</u> = to free from confinement, bondage, obligation, pain, etc.; let go; to free from anything that restrains, fastens, etc.

<u>Responsibility</u> = the act of being answerable or accountable for that which has been entrusted into one's power, control, management, or care; chargeable for decisions made or stewardship of one's authority or power; reliable or dependable in conducting that for which one is responsible and accountable.

<u>Aware</u> = means "having knowledge; conscious; cognizant; informed; alert; knowledgeable."

1. Awareness. *(**1 Corinthians 10:11, 13; Jeremiah 17:9; Psalm 139; Jude 24-25.**)*

    (a.) At this stage, the believer should be a spiritual person with a spiritual mind, who has the knowledge of God and His will, and is conscious and cognizant with some spiritual discernment. The young man is an informed and alert saint of God, who can now make some intelligent decisions based upon the Word of God and not his feelings or emotions.

2. Awareness of strength and weaknesses; harness flesh while dealing with and confronting weaknesses honestly and with total dependence upon God.

    (a.) The young man is very much aware and alert to his vigor, mental power, firmness, courage, and power by reason of influence or authority. But he is also very conscious and cognizant of his feebleness and lack of strength in certain area(s) of his life and of his inadequate or defective qualities in his character.

"Young men are strong. But fathers know the way."
"Young men may know the rules, but fathers know the exceptions."

   (b.) The young man has learned how to harness *(to bring under subjection his flesh and gain control over his fleshly appetites and cravings for effective use as an instrument of God and for living a victorious life daily as an overcomer)* his flesh. He doesn't deny his private struggles in his own flesh but deal with them honestly – depending on God for grace and victory.

   (c.) The young man knows that the greatest conflict he has and is engaged in is within him between the Spirit and the flesh (Galatians 5:16-23). He knows the importance of having a transformed mind and the mind of Christ, and that the battlefield is the mind (Romans 12:1-2; Ephesians 4:20-24; Philippians 2:5-8).

3. Awareness of character: modeling a godly character & being an example.

   (a.) The young man has become a follower of Christ, his Master and Lord, and he models the moral and ethical quality of Jesus Christ. *(1 Corinthians 11:1; John 13:12-17.)*

   (b.) He does not seek to make a reputation for himself. He desires to manifest the life of Christ within him, that men may be drawn to Him [Christ], Who is the hope of glory. *(Matthew 5:16; Galatians 2:20; 4:19.)*

4. Awareness of acceptance [in Christ] and avoidance [of evil].

   (a.) The young man does not look for acceptance by people. He has come to believe and know that he has been accepted in the Beloved, Jesus Christ. *(Ephesians 1:3-6) He is not a men pleaser. At all times, he seeks to please God rather than men, even though he would like to please men, especially when it pleases God. But he does seek to please men at the expense of pleasing his God. (Galatians 1:10; Romans 15:1-3.)*

   (b.) The young man has come to fear the LORD. There fore, he avoids evil and sin and even the very appear ance of evil. *(Job 1:1; 2:3; 1 Thessalonians 5:22; Matthew 6:13.)*

   (c.) He knows that he has been made righteous in Christ through faith. Therefore, if he should fall (and the righteous do sometimes), he will get back up again. *(Proverbs 24:16; 1 John 1:7-9.)*

5. Awareness of adversary: identifying, recognizing, and over coming the adversary. The apostle John said three things about the young man: (1) he is strong; (2) God's word lives

in him; and (3) he has won the victory over the evil one (1 John 2:13b, 14b).

Take notice where the young men strength came from. It came from his abiding and continuing in the Word of God! He found strength in the Word (Acts 20:32; Psalm 119:28). The young man knows and understands that "Man does not live by bread alone, but by every word that proceeds out of the mouth of God" (Matthew 4:4).

The young man knows and understands that we [the believers in Jesus Christ] have a real adversary called Satan, the Devil. Therefore, he knows that he cannot afford to give place to him, live to satisfy the flesh, and not be of a sober mind at all times. He must "watch" and "pray" so that he will not become a prey of the adversary. **(1 Peter 5:8-10; Ephesians 6:10-16; James 4:7; Revelation 12:7-11.)**

The young man must have at least three things:

1.) <u>Determination:</u> He must have at this stage, come to a decision or of fixing his heart and settling his mind to purposefully serve the Lord faithfully and without compromise. By now, he has arrived at a fixed purpose or intention about Christ and his walk with the Lord. He has a fixed direction toward reaching the goal, the mark, and the prize that is supreme and heavenly. *(Psalm 57:7; 108:1; 112:7; Philippians 3:7-21.)*

2.) <u>Persistence/Perseverance:</u> He possesses an enduring tenacity that causes him to persevere in spite of opposition, obstacles, discouragement, etc. He is constant in his walk with God, and has continuity – lasting to the end. He has learned to persist in his undertaking to be a disciple of Jesus Christ and maintain a purpose and a cause that sustain him in spite of difficulty and persecution and offenses that will come to distract you and tempt you to give up. *(2Timothy 2:3; 2 Corinthians 4:8-12, 15-17; 6:3-10; Luke 21:19, 25-28; Matthew 24:13.)*

3.) <u>Knowledge</u> (to overcome the danger of ignorance):

Knowledge is power and light. Believers cannot afford to be ignorant, or to remain in ignorance. Ignorance doesn't mean that one is stupid. It simply means that you are lacking in knowledge, especially the knowledge of God and His will. Satan is counting on the believer's ignorance for his advantage: ignorance of God, of Christ, of God's will, of who you are, of what you possess, and of what authority you have as a believer. *(Hosea 4:6; 6:1-3; 2 Corinthians 2:10-11; Ephesians 5:15-17; Colossians 1:9-13.)*

STAGE FOUR

FATHER/ADULT STAGE: (Trusting Stage)

"I am writing to you, <u>fathers</u>, because you know Him Who has been from the beginning."(1 John 2:13a, 14a, NASB)

"I am writing to you, <u>fathers</u>, because you know Christ Who has existed from the beginning." (GW)

"I am writing to you, <u>fathers</u>, because you have come to know (recognize, be aware of, and understand) Him Who [has existed] from the beginning."(Amplified Bible)

<u>Know</u> = is the Greek word *"ginosko"*, <u>*ghin-oce'ko*</u>. It means "come to know" and connotes a knowledge that is learned through experience [an instance or process of personally encountering or undergoing something] (John 8:32; 1 John 2:13a, 14a).[9]

(1.)   Another Greek word for "know" is *"eido"*, <u>*i'do*</u>. It means "properly to see; by implication to know: - be aware, behold, (have) knowledge of, perceive, be sure, tell, or understand." (Romans 8:28)[10]

(2.)   Webster defines "know" as "to perceive or understand as fact or truth; to apprehend clearly and with certainty; be (well) acquainted with."

Fathers are those who have come to full maturity in Christ, and who totally rest in, recline on, trust in, and depend on the Father in heaven, as they allow the peace of God through Jesus Christ to guard their hearts and minds. They have complete trust in God, that <u>is, mature faith</u> in Him (Mark 11:22). The problem is that we don't

9 Strong's Hebrew Greek Concordance
10 Ibid

have many believers in Christ who are *"fathers"*, or who have come to and reach this level of spiritual growth and maturity. Make it your goal to become a *"father" spiritually* in the Lord!

Here are some characteristics of fathers:

1. Relationships [right relationships; true covenant relationships]: Fathers understand that everything that has to do with God the Father in heaven, the Kingdom, and the Church is about *"relationship"*: salvation, being members together of the body of Christ, being citizens together of the Kingdom of God, being in covenant, etc. (John 1:12; 15:1-8; 1 Corinthians 12:14-27.)

    (a.) *"Relationship"* is a connection between persons by blood, marriage, covenant, association, or involvement. "Fathers" are truly connected, and they understand the importance of maintaining proper and right relationships. As a matter of fact, they place a tremendous value on relationship and the maintenance of a healthy godly relationship.

    (b.) "Fathers" understand that it is not enough just to know the Father and be rightly related to Him; he knows that he must be rightly related to his brother in the Lord (Matthew 5:21-26; Philippians 4:3).

2. Responsible (accountable; good steward; take responsibility for choices; no blame game):

    (a.) *"Fathers"* don't mind being held accountable for that which they are responsible. They do not run from responsibility or accountability.

    (b.) *"Fathers"* are good stewards or managers of all that has been committed into their trust, even the mysteries of God (1 Corinthians 4:1-5).

3. Restful resolve:

   (a.) *"Fathers"* have learned how to rest in God and to be content in every situation (Psalm 37:1-9; 27:13-14; Philippians 4:11-13). The things that use to shake them, cause them to doubt and fear, or cause their minds to be agitated, disturbed, and robbed of the peace of God no longer moves them (Acts 20:22-25; John 14:1, 27; 16:33).

   (b.) *"Fathers"* are those who are free from anything that wearies, troubles, or disturbs the mind. They possess, as their personal possession through Christ, both spiritual and mental calm. They are at rest in the Lord and in their minds. They experience the peace of God (Romans 5:1-5; Philippians 4:4-9), being at rest – at peace, as well as the refreshing quiet, tranquility, and peaceful state of mind.

   (c.) *"Fathers"* can experience such freedom and relief of mind from those things that will disturb and agitate the mind, because they have come to a definite and earnest decision and determination about putting their total trust in God and trusting Him at all times, in every situation, and in everything (Psalm 9:10; 25:2; 33:21; 56:3, 4, 11; 62:8; Romans 8:28).

4. Restorer/Repairer (restoring the fallen and all things of God):

   (a.) *"Fathers"* are spiritual and mature saints of God who know how to restore their fallen brethren in the spirit of meekness (Galatians 6:1-5). We do fall sometimes, even without planning to fall (Proverbs 24:16). The fallen righteous brother or sister in Christ needs to be restored by those who are spiritual, doing unto them what you would want done unto you, if (or when) you fall.

- (b.) *"Fathers"* are also repairer of the breach, relationships, communities, etc., and they take the initiative to bring things back into divine order. They know that they are called to be men or women [because this has nothing to do with gender here] who makes amend for or make good for the wrong or damage done. *"Fathers"* or the *"spiritual believers"* are the remedy for restoration; and they allow the Spirit of God to use and work through them to restore to a good, sound and healthy condition or state that which was damaged, defected, or decayed [relationships, churches, friendships, truths, doctrines, misunderstandings, miscommunications, etc.] (Isaiah 58:12-14).

- (c.) They understand the ministry of reconciliation that we have been given by the Lord (2 Corinthians 5:18-21).

5. Rejoicing and reward (a place of):

- (a.) *"Fathers"* are those who know how to rejoice at all times, whether the times are good or bad (Philippians 1:18; 2:16-18; 3:1, 3; 4:4). He rejoices because of Whom he has believed and put his trust, and because he knows what his God is able to do (2 Timothy 1:12). He has learned not to allow the negative circumstances or situations to dictate his praise of his God and Father in heaven through Yeshua. He knows how to give thanks in everything (1 Thessalonians 5:18).

- (b.) *"Fathers"* also know and understand that loyalty to the Lord and patient endurance will always be rewarded by God in the end. He knows that God Himself will compensate or recompense him for his service given, and hardships endured (Mark 10:29-31; James 1:12). So, he doesn't look for all that God will reward him in the here and now.

CONCLUSION

To grow is normal. To not grow is abnormal, even in the spiritual realm. The process is the same. We grow and go from one stage or level to another; and the next level we transition to is different from the one we left. Childhood is different from infancy. Adolescent is different from childhood. The young man is different from adolescent. The father stage is different from the young man. Each level must be walked out and completed before one can rise to the next level or stage.

It is the Father's will that we do not remain children who are tossed by every wind of doctrine that men may teach. He wants us to become a "perfect man", that is, a full-grown or mature man, and arrive at really mature manhood in Christ and in our character. It is a process of progression that begins at one point, state, stage or level, and ends at the place, level, stage or state that God has so willed and ordained. We must never settle or become content to remain on a level or at a stage that is not the perfect will of God.

The sad truth is that we do not have many believers in Christ who have truly arrived at really mature manhood and have become fathers [spiritually in their growth, development, and manhood – 1 Corinthians 13:11]. Many believers don't even know the depth of the intimacy and fellowship that can be experience in our relationship with the Father. Only "fathers" really know Him. This "knowing" only comes through experience and not knowledge alone. Job said on the other side of his great trials and suffering, "I had heard about You with the hearing of the ear, but now my spiritual eyes see You [and your salvation, power and glory]" (Job 42:5).

My will is the will of God. Like Yeshua [Jesus], my meat is to do the will of Him who called and saved me (John 4:34). Your will should also be to do the will of God. We desire that every true believer and disciple of Jesus Christ that God plants in the house of the LORD and set in the Community of the Lord come to full age, full manhood, and full maturity in Christ. It is our will and heart's desire that you be a sheep of the Lord, who knows his or her Good Shepherd in a personal intimate way as you walk close to Him, maintaining constant vibrant and unbroken fellowship with Him. Be sheep who **hear, know, recognize,** and **follow** the voice of the Good Shepherd and not the voice of a stranger or hireling! Read – <u>John 10:11-16;</u>

<u>Hebrews 5:11-6:2 says:</u>

"I have a lot more to say about this, but it is hard to get it across to you since you've picked up this bad habit of not listening. By this time you ought to beteachers yourselves, yet here I find you need someone to sit down with you andgo over the basics on God's again, starting from square one – baby's milk, whenyou should have been on solid food long ago! Milk is for beginners, inexperiencedin God's ways; solid food is for the mature, who have some practice in telling right from wrong. So come on, let's leave the preschool finger-painting exercises on Christ and get on with the grand work of art. **Grow up in Christ!** *(Message Bible)*

I personally like this translation, because it depicts the very essence of this book.

Notes

Notes

Notes

REFERENCES

Preface:

[1] Adam Clark Commentary, Matthew 23:23, Joyce Myers Ministries Bible Software: The Everyday Life Bible Study Library. WORDSearch. 2009.

[2] Ibid.

Stages Overview:

[3] Strong's Hebrew Greek Concordance, Joyce Myers Ministries Bible Software: The Everyday Life Bible Study Library. WORDSearch. 2009.

[4] Adam Clark Commentary, Joyce Myers Ministries Bible Software: The Every day Life Bible Study Library. WORDSearch. 2009.

[5] MacDonald, William. The Believer's Bible Commentary. Nashville, Tennessee: Thomas Nelson Publishers, Inc., 1995.

Infant Stage (Provision Stage):

[6] Spangler, Ann and Tverberg, Lois. Sitting at the Feet of Rabbi Jesus. Grand Rapids, Michigan: Zondervan, 2009.

Childhood Stage (Identity Stage):

[7] Gilbrant, Thoralf and Lint, Gregory A. The Complete Biblical Library. Salem, Virginia: World Library Press, Inc., 2000.

[8] Strong's Hebrew Greek Concordance, Joyce Myers Ministries Bible Software: The Everyday Life Bible Study Library. WORDSearch. 2009.

Father/ Adult Stage (Trusting Stage):

[9 & 10] Strong's Hebrew Greek Concordance, Joyce Myers Ministries Bible Software: The Everyday Life Bible Study Library. WORDSearch. 2009.

Words defined in the following sections: Objectives, Stages Overview, Stage One: Infant Stage, Stage Two: The Childhood Stage, and Stage Four: The father/Adult Stage) are from Dictionary.com, LLC (Dictionary.com, Dictionary and Thesaurus for IPAD; © 2013 Dictionary.com, LLC. Updated December 18, 2013.